MOHAMMAD IBRAHIM ZAUQ
THE MUGHAL SUFI POET-LAUREATE
Selected Poems

For a list and descriptions of our over 400 titles
go to www.newhumanitybooks.com
or on Amazon go to
http://www.amazon.com/Paul-Smith/e/B00CL10PQU/ref=nttdpepwbko

MOHAMMAD IBRAHIM ZAUQ

THE MUGHAL SUFI POET-LAUREATE
Selected Poems

Translation & Introduction

Paul Smith

NEW HUMANITY BOOKS
BOOK HEAVEN
Booksellers & Publishers

NEW HUMANITY BOOKS

BOOK HEAVEN

(Booksellers & Publishers for over 40 years)

47 Main Road

Campbells Creek

Victoria 3451 Australia

Urdu Poetry/Mysticism/Sufism/Islamic Literature/

www.newhumanitybooks.com

ISBN-13: 978-1987566116

CONTENTS

The Life & Poetry & Times of Zauq... 7

Selected Bibliography... 12

Sufism in Poetry... 13

Some of the Poetic Forms Used by Zauq... 39

Ghazals... 51

Ruba'is... 93

Qit'as... 103

Qasida... 121

Sher (Rhyming Couplets)... 131

The Life & Poetry & Times of Zauq

Mohammad Ibrahim took Zauq (meaning 'taste') as his *takhallus* or pen-name. He was born at Delhi in 1788. His father was a lowly paid soldier. Zauq, not having proper treatment on account of the poverty of his family survived attacks of small-pox *nine times* during his childhood.

He was sent to a *maktab* (elementary religious school) run by Hafiz Ghulam Rasool who was a poet. Under his influence the boy also became attracted to poetry.

Shah Naseer was the most famous master poet of Delhi at that time. Zauq began showing his *ghazals* to him. Naseer recognised natural talent and made him his pupil. Gradually, Zauq began participating in readings. His natural way with poetry and his obsession to excel in it eventually brought fame and fortune.

He was a prominent contemporary of Ghalib and in the history of Urdu poetry the rivalry of the two is well known and during his lifetime Zauq was more popular than his now much more famous rival.

He was a religious man and in his *ghazals* he often dealt with mystical (Sufi) and ethical themes. Most of his poetical output was lost during the mutiny of 1857. He had passed away two years earlier in 1855. What remains is twelve hundred couplets of *ghazals* and *ruba'is* and fifteen eulogies.

One of the greatest Urdu poets of all times, Mohammad Ibrahim Zauq is regarded as one of the pioneers of Urdu poetry. He was born in 1789 in a poor family and had a very ordinary education. Yet his treasure of Urdu poem and ghazals were immense and are considered priceless today. Zauq was the pen name of Sheikh Mohammad Ibrahim and he composed his *ghazals* and poems under this pseudonym. In his later years, he went on to learn some tradition, history and astrology. Most of his brilliant compositions were lost during the wars fought for India's independence. Yet, he left behind numerous compositions and a rich legacy of *ghazals, mukhammus* and many poems. To know more about Zauq, continue to read this insightful biography on him.

Zauq's father Shaikh Mohammed Ramzan was a lowly placed soldier in the Mughal army. This meant that Zauq did not have proper means to grow up with. He fell prey to small pox when he was a little child, but miraculously survived it even though his family did not even have enough money to get him properly treated. He was not sent to a fancy school like his contemporaries but instead went to a religious school. Elementary religious schools were called *maktab* in those times. This particular school that Zauq went to was run by Hafiz Ghulam Rasool. He himself was a poet and used Shauq as his pen name. it was mainly under his influence that Zauq took liking to Urdu poetry in his young age. It was Hafiz who suggested the nom de plume of Zauq to young Mohammad Ibrahim. He guided him and took him as a pupil in poetry. Zauq did not finish his schooling and got hooked to poetry instead. He started showing his *ghazals* to Shah Naseer, a popular poet of his times. He took suggestions from him and Naseer found Zauq to be really talented. Naseer took Zauq under his guidance. It was Zauq's singular hard work and passion towards poetry that made him so successful and famous. There came a time when Zauq started to get more popularity than Naseer. This infuriated Naseer and he banned his entry into his group. This did not affect Zauq's passion and he continued to rely on his natural talent and kept writing and reciting poetry. His poet friend Meer Kazim Husain Beqarar was working in the royal court as a mentor to the young Crown Prince Zafar. It was through him that Zauq got entry into the royal court and he started to take part in royal mushairas. Later, Beqarar took up the job of royal accountant in the court and Zauq got the opportunity to mentor Zafar.

He was paid 4 rupees as his monthly salary but later it was raised up to 100 rupees. He died as the poet laureate in the Mughal Court.

Zauq's poetry is appreciated because of his impeccable control of the language and composition of poetry quite smoothly even under difficult meter. He was a poet at the royal court since a very young age and he was supposed to write poetry that would praise and appreciate the royalty, in order to benefit some profit from the emperor. He is still considered to be a great eulogy writer as much of his job as a court poet was to write eloquent eulogies. Bahadur Shah Zafar was a fan of simplicity in the language used in poetry; therefore Zauq used simple words, phrases, diction, sentences in his poetry. Even the similes used in his poetry were very simple, takes from the common surrounding culture. His poetry was also famous at the time for its spontaneity. He also used the subject of religion and ethics in his poetry because he was a deeply religious man. Therefore, sometimes his poetry sounds less melodious and preachier.

He was considered as a rival to none other than Mirza Ghalib. Though he wasn't a great philosopher as Ghalib, yet the respect he acquired in his lifetime is commendable. Zauq died in the year of 1854 as a poet laureate, in Delhi. His grave is in the Paharganj area in Delhi. It is said that his resident was also nearby that area on Nabi Karim but it was never really identified. His grave was only restored under the orders of the Supreme Court.

Selected Bibliography

Kulliaat-e-Zauq, edited by Dr. Tanweer Ahmed Alavi, Majlise Taraqqi Adab, Lahore, 1964.

Zauq: Life & Poems, Translation & Introduction Paul Smith, New Humanity Books, Campbells Creek 2016.

Zauq: Sufi Poet-Laureate & Spiritual Master of the Las Mughal Emperor, the Sufi Poet Zafar: Translation & Introduction Paul Smith, New Humanity Books, Campbells Creek 2016.

Urdu Ghazals: An Anthology From the 16th to 20th Century. K.C. Kanda. Sterling Pub. New Delhi 1995. *(Pages 126-137).*

Urdu Poetry: An Anthology up to 19th Century : Translated & Romanised into English by Shah Abdus Salam. BR Publications, Delhi *(Pages 240-9).*

Masterpieces of Urdu Rubaiyat by K.C. Kanda. Sterling Paperbacks, New Delhi, 1995. *(Pages 56-61).*

Glimpses of Urdu Poetry: Text, Translation and Transliteration by K.C. Kanda, Lotus Press, New Delhi 2007. *(Page 51-59, 395-397).*

The Golden Tradition: An Anthology of Urdu Poetry... Selected, Translated and with an Introduction by Ahmed Ali, Columbia University Press, New York, 1973. *(Pages 217-221).*

Shimmering Jewels: Anthology of Poetry Under the Reigns of the Mughal Emperors of India (1526-1857) Translations & Introduction by Paul Smith, New Humanity Books, Campbells Creek, 2012.

Bahadur Shah Zafar: Sufi Poet & Last Mughal Emperor & his Circle of Poets... Zauq, Ghalib, Momin, Shefta, Dagh: Selected Poems, Translations & Introduction by Paul Smith, New Humanity Books, Campbells Creek, 2017. *(Pages 123-149).*

A Treasury of Urdu Poetry, From Mir to Faiz. Selected and Translated by Kuldip Salil, Rajpal& Sons, Delhi, 2015. *(Pp. 69-71).*

The Book of Urdu Sufi Poets, Translations & Introduction by Paul Smith, New Humanity Books, 2016 *(Pages 159-167)*

Masterpieces of Urdu Ruba'iyat Translatred by K.C. Kanda, Sterling Paperbacks, New Delhi, 1995. *(Pages 57-63)*

https://rekhta.org/poets/sheikh-ibrahim-zauq/ghazals

Wikipedia article

Sufism in Poetry

It has been said that Adam was the first Sufi and Perfect Master (*Qutub*) and that he was also the first poet as he named everything and so through his 'Adamic Alphabet' (see the *Hebraic Tongue Restored* by Fabre D'Olivet) all languages were born and so... all poetry. Two of Arabia's most highly regarded scholars of the poetic form also claim he was the father of the poetic form of the *ghazal*... the form most used by Sufi and Dervish poets up to the present day.

Sufism is said by many Masters and authors to have always existed since Adam as the esoteric side of each faith that has begun by an appearance of that original Perfect Master coming back as the *Rasool*, Prophet, Messiah, Avatar, Buddha, etc., whatever that Divine One is called.

Many Perfect Masters (*Qutubs*) were poets and many were not. Many came after the appearance of the Prophet Mohammed and many came before him. But, Sufis and Dervishes were called by those names after he passed from this world. The first 'Sufi' or 'Dervish' is probably Mohammed's son-in-law Hazrat Ali who composed one of the first *ghazals* ever recorded that essentially sums up the meaning of Sufism and Dervishness...

You do not know it, but in you is the remedy;

you cause the sickness, but this you don't see.

You are but a small form... this, you assume:

but you're larger than any universe, in reality.

You are the book that of any fallacies is clear,

in you are all letters spelling out, the mystery.

You are the Being, you're the very Being... It:

you contain That, which contained cannot be!

I have used both the terms 'Sufi' and 'Dervish' in this book because Amir Khusrau was called a 'Sufi' by others but probably saw himself more as a 'Dervish', for... during the time that he was alive, many 'Sufis' had become corrupt and were following false masters. Hafiz likewise always called himself a Dervish and often when mentioning Sufis in his poetry it was usually to criticize them. During his lifetime in Shiraz there was an extremist Sufi Order led by a false master Shaikh Ali Kolah who sided with various dictators and subjected the people to a very vicious brand of fundamentalism. By the 13th Century many Sufi Orders had become corrupt and full of various dogmas, useless rituals and power hungry and hypocritical shaikhs and false masters.

Those who called themselves 'Dervishes' then really meant 'true Sufis'.

The first Sufi and Dervish poets composed in Arabic even though some of them, including the famous and infamous Sufi martyr Mansur al-Hallaj were originally from Persia... he was from near Shiraz. From the 10th to the 17th century the vast majority of Sufi and Dervish and other poets in the region composed in Persian, a few in the new languages of Turkish and Urdu and some in Hindi; after that... the languages most used by the most conscious and influential poets were Urdu, Punjabi and Sindhi, as the stream of God-consciousness moved originally from Arabia and Egypt to Iraq and Syria then into Iran and Afghanistan and Turkey and finally into the Indian Sub-Continent.

To follow this golden thread of Spiritual Poetry one must follow the true Spiritual Hierarchy of real Saints and God-realized Souls... Perfect Masters, their lives and stories are to be found in the many books listed below and in many others.

What is the essential belief and philosophy of the Sufi and Dervish Masters and Poets? To put it as simply as possibly... The Love of God, the belief in God in human form, the love and respect for all of God's Creation and to try to not hurt anyone or thing. And of course a belief in Truth, Love and Beauty as the greatest of the Divine Attributes. A belief similar, if not the same as the Christian Mystics and Vedantists and believers in the inner way of most religions.

Hazrat Inayat Khan says in his essay on Sufi Poetry: "There is a saying that a poet is a prophet, and this saying has a great significance and a hidden meaning. There is no doubt that though poetry is not necessarily prophecy, prophecy is born in poetry. If one were to say that poetry is a body which is adopted by the spirit of prophecy, it would not be wrong. Wagner has said that noise is not necessarily music, and the same thing can be said in connection with poetry: that a verse written in rhyme and metre is not necessarily true poetry. Poetry is an art, a music expressed in the beauty and harmony of words. No doubt much of the poetry one reads is meant either as a pastime or for amusement, but real poetry comes from the dancing of the soul. And no one can make the soul dance unless the soul itself is inclined to dance. Also, no soul can dance which is not alive.

In the Bible it is said that no one will enter the kingdom of God whose soul is not born again, and being born means being alive. It is not only a happy disposition or an external inclination to merriment and pleasure that is the sign of a living soul; for external joy and amusement may come simply through the external being of man, although even in this outer joy and happiness there is a glimpse of the inner joy and happiness which is the sign of the soul having been born again. What makes it alive? It makes itself alive when it strikes its depths instead of reaching outward. The soul, after coming up against the iron wall of this life of falsehood, turns back within itself, it encounters itself, and this is how it becomes living.

In order to make this idea more clear I should like to take as an example a man who goes out into the world; a man with thought, with feeling, with energy, with desire, with ambition, with enthusiasm to live and work in life. And because of the actual nature of life, his experience will make him feel constantly up against an iron wall in whatever direction he strikes out. And the nature of man is such that when he meets with an obstacle then he struggles; he lives in the outer life, and he goes on struggling. He does not know any other part of life, for he lives only on the surface. But then there is another man who is sensitive because he has a sympathetic and tender heart, and every blow coming from the outer world, instead of making him want to hit back out-wardly, makes him want to strike at himself inwardly. And the consequence of this is that his soul, which after being born on this earth seems to be living but in reality is in a grave, becomes awakened by that action; and when once the soul is awakened in this way it expresses itself outwardly, whether in music, in art, in poetry, m action, or in whatever way it wishes to express itself.

In this way a poet is born. There are two signs which reveal the poet: one sign is imagination, the other is feeling, and both are essential on the spiritual path. A man, however learned and good, who yet lacks these two qualities, can never arrive at a satisfactory result, especially on the spiritual path.

The sacred scriptures of all ages, whether of the Hindus or the Parsis, the race of Ben Israel or of others, were all given in poetry or in poetic prose. No spiritual person however great, however pious and spiritually advanced, has ever been able to give a scripture to the world unless he was blessed with the gift of poetry. One may ask if this would still be possible nowadays, when sentiment takes second place in life's affairs and people wish everything to be expressed plainly, 'cut and dried' as the saying is, and when one has become so accustomed to having everything, especially in science, explained in clear words. But it must be understood that facts about the names and forms of this world may be scientifically explained in plain words, but when one wishes to interpret the sensation one gets when looking at life, it cannot be explained except m the way that the prophets did in poetry. No one has ever explained nor can anyone ever explain the truth in words. Language exists only for the convenience of everyday affairs; the deepest sentiments cannot be explained in words. The message that the prophets have given to the world at different times is an interpretation in their own words of the idea of life that they have received.

Inspiration begins in poetry and culminates in prophecy. One can picture the poet as a soul which has so to speak risen from its grave and is beginning to make graceful movements; but when the same soul begins to move and to dance in all directions and to touch heaven and earth in its dance, expressing all the beauty it sees -- that is prophecy. The poet when he is developed reads the mind of the universe, although it very often happens that the poet himself does not know the real meaning of what he has said. Very often one finds that a poet has said something, and after many years there comes a moment when he realizes the true meaning of what he said. And this shows that behind all these different activities the divine Spirit is hidden, and the divine Spirit often manifests through an individual without his realizing that it is divine.

In the East the prophet is called *Payghambar*, which means the Messenger, the one who carries somebody's word to someone else. In reality every individual in this world is the medium of an impulse which is hidden behind him, and that impulse he gives out, mostly without knowing it. This is not only so with living beings, but one can see it even in objects; for every object has its purpose, and by fulfilling its purpose that object is fulfilling the scheme of nature. Therefore whatever be the line or activity of a man, whether it is: business or science or music or art or poetry, he is a medium in some way or other. There are mediums of living beings, there are mediums of those who have passed to the other side, and there are mediums that represent their country, their nation, their race. Every individual is acting in his own way as a medium.

When the prophet or the poet dives deep into himself he touches that perfection which is the source and goal of all beings. And as an electric wire connected with a battery receives the force or energy of the battery, so the poet who has touched the innermost depths of his being has touched the perfect God, and from there he derives that wisdom, that beauty, and that power which belong to the perfect Self of God. There is no doubt that in all things there is the real and the false and there is the raw and the ripe. Poetry comes from the tendency to contemplation. A man with imagination cannot retain the imagination, cannot mould it, cannot build it up unless he has this contemplative tendency within him. The more one contemplates the more one is able to conceive of what one receives. Not only this, but after contemplation a person is able to realize a certain idea more clearly than if that idea had only passed through his mind.

The process of contemplation is like the work of the camera: when the camera is put before a certain object and has been properly focused, then only that object is received by the camera. And therefore when an object before one is limited, then one can see that object more clearly. What constitutes the appeal of the poet is that he tells his readers of something he has seen behind these generally recognized ideas. The prophet goes still further. He not only contemplates one idea, but he can contemplate on any idea: There comes a time in the life of the prophet or of anyone who contemplates, when whatever object he casts his glance upon opens up and reveals to him what it has in its heart. In the history of the world we see that besides their great imagination, their great dreams, their ecstasy and their joy in the divine life, the prophets have often been great reformers, scientists, medical men or even statesmen.

This in itself shows their balance; it shows that theirs is not a one-sided development; they do not merely become dreamers or go into trances, but both sides of their personality are equally development. It is an example of God in man that the prophets manifest. We can see this in the life of Joseph: we are told that he was so innocent, so simple that he went with his brothers, yielding to them, and that this led to his betrayal. In his relationship with Zuleikha we see the human being, the tendency to beauty. And at the same time there is the question he continually asks: What am I doing? What shall I do? Later in his life we see him as one who knows the secret of dreams, as the mystic who interprets the dream of the king. And still later in his life we see that he became a minister, with the administration of the country in his hands, able to carry out the work of the state.

Spirituality has become far removed from material life, and so God is far removed from humanity. Therefore one cannot any more conceive of God speaking through a man, through someone like oneself even a religious man who reads the Bible every day will have great difficulty in understanding the verse, 'Be ye perfect, even as your Father in heaven is perfect.' The Sufi message and its mission are to bring this truth to the consciousness of the world: that man can dive so deep within himself that he can touch the depths where he is united with the whole of life, with all souls, and that he can derive from that source harmony, beauty, peace, and power.

Sufi poetic imagery stands by itself, distinct and peculiar in its character. It is both admired and criticized for its peculiarity. Why it is different from the expressions of other poets born in various countries, is because of its Persian origin and the particular qualities of Persia - the fine climate, the ancient traditions, its being the place where, it is said, wine was tasted for the first time; a land of luxury, a land of beauty, a land of art and imagination. It was natural that with Persian thinkers of all periods, who thought deeply on life, its nature and character, their expressions should become subtle, artistic, fine, and picturesque. In short, it is the dancing of the soul. In all other living beings, the soul is lying asleep, but when once the soul has awakened, called by beauty, it leaps up dancing, and its every movement makes a picture, whether in writing, poetry, music or whatever it may be. A dancing soul will always express the most subtle and intricate harmonies in the realm of music or poetry.

When we read the works of Hafiz and of many other Sufi poets, we shall find that they are full of the same imagery and this is partly because that was the time of Islam. The mission of Islam had a particular object in view, and in order to attain that object it had strict rules about life. A free-thinker had difficulty in expressing his thoughts without being accused of having done a great wrong towards the religion and the State. And these free- thinkers of Persia, with their dancing soul and continual enthusiasm, began to express their soul in this particular imagery, using words such as 'the beloved', 'wine', 'wine-press', and 'tavern'. And this poetry became so popular that not only the wise derived benefit from it, but also the simple ones enjoyed the beauty of its wonderful expressions which make an immediate appeal to every soul. There is no doubt that the souls which were already awakened and those on the point of awakening were inspired by these poems. Souls which were opening their eyes after the deep slumber of many years began to rise up and dance; as Hafiz says, 'If those pious ones of long robes listen to my verse, my song, they will immediately begin to get up and dance'. And then he says at the end of the poem, 'Forgive me, O pious ones, for I am drunk just now!'

This concept of drinking is used in various connections and conveys many different meanings. In the first place, imagine that there is a magic tavern where there are many different kinds of wine. Each wine has a different effect upon the person who drinks it. One drinks a wine which makes him light-hearted, frivolous, humorous; another drinks a wine which makes him sympathetic, kind, tender, gentle. Someone else drinks one which makes him bewildered at everything he sees. Another drinks and finds his way into the ditch. One becomes angry after drinking while another becomes passionate. One drinks and is drowned in despair. Another drinks and begins to feel loving and affectionate; yet another drinks a wine that makes him discouraged with everything. Imagine how interested we should all be to see that tavern! In point of fact we live in that tavern and we see it every day; only, we do not take proper notice of it.

Once I saw a Madzub, (one who is absorbed in a plane of involving consciousness) a man who pretends to be insane, who though living in the world does not wish to be of the world, standing in the street of a large city, laughing. I stood there, feeling curious to know what made him laugh at that moment. And I understood that it was the sight of so many drunken men, each one having had his particular wine.

It is most amusing when we look at it in this way. There is not one single being on earth who does not drink wine; only, the wine of one is different from the wine of the other. A man does not only drink during the day but the whole night long, and he awakens in the morning intoxicated by whatever wine he has been drinking. He awakens with fear or with anger, he awakens with joy, or with love and affection; and the moment he awakens from sleep he shows what wine he has been drinking.

One might ask why the great Sufi teachers have taken such a great interest in the particular imagery of these poets. The reason is that they found the solution to the problem of life by looking upon the world as a tavern, with many wines and each person drinking a different one. They discovered the alchemy, the chemical process, by which to change the wine that a person drinks, and give him another wine to see how this works. The work of the Sufi teacher with his pupil is of that kind. He first finds out which blend of wine his *mureed* (disciple) drinks, and then he finds out which blend be must have.

But, one will ask, is there then no place for soberness in life? There is, but when that soberness is properly interpreted, one sees that it too is wine. Amir(Khusraw), the Hindustani poet, has expressed it in verse, 'The eyes of the sober one spoke to the eyes of the drunken one: "You have no place here, for your intoxication is different from mine."' The awakened person seems to be asleep to the sleeping one, and so the one who has become sober also appears to be still drunk; for the condition of life is such that no one appears to be sober. It is this soberness which is called *Nirvana* by Buddhists and *Mukti* by Hindus. But if I were asked if it is then desirable for me to be sober, my reply would be, no. What is desirable is for us to know whet soberness is, and after knowing what soberness is, then to take any wine we may choose. The tavern is there; wines are there. There are two men: one who is the master of wine, the other who is the slave of wine; the first drinks wine, but wine drinks up the other. The one whom wine drinks up is mortal; he who drinks wine becomes immortal. What is the love of God? What is divine knowledge? Is it not a wine? Its experience is different, its intoxication is different, for there is ordinary wine and there is most costly champagne. The difference is in the wine.

In the imagery of the Sufi poets this tavern (winehouse) is the world, and the Saki (Winebringer) is God. In whatever form the wine-giver comes and gives a wine, it is God who comes. In this way, by recognizing the Saki, the wine-giver, in all forms, the Sufi worships God; for he recognizes Him in friend and foe as the wine-giver. And wine is that influence which we receive *from* life, an harmonious influence or a depressing influence, a beautiful influence or one that lacks beauty. When we have given in to it then we become drunk, then we become addicted to it, then we are under its influence; but when we have sought soberness then we have risen above it all, and then all wines are ours.

At all times Persia has had great poets and it has been called the land of poetry; in the first place because the Persian language is so well adapted to poetry, but also because all Persian poetry contains a mystical touch. The literary value of the poetry only makes it poetry; but when a mystical value is added this makes the poetry prophecy. The climate and atmosphere of Persia have also been most helpful to poetry, and the very imaginative nature of the people has made their poetry rich. At all times and in all countries, when the imagination has no scope for expansion, poetry dies and materialism increases.

There is no poet in the world who is not a mystic. A poet is a mystic whether consciously, or unconsciously, for no one can write poetry without inspiration, and when a poet touches the profound depths of the spirit, struck by some aspect of life, he brings forth a poem as a diver brings forth a pearl.

In this age of materialism and ever-growing commercialism man seems to have lost the way of inspiration. During my travels I was asked by a well-known writer whether it is really true that there is such a thing as inspiration. This gave me an idea of how far nowadays some writers and poets are removed from inspiration. It is the materialism of the age which is responsible for this; if a person has a tendency towards poetry or music, as soon as he begins to write something his first thought is, 'Will it catch on or not? What will be its practical value?' And generally what catches on is that which appeals to the average man. In this way culture is going downward instead of upward.

When the soul of the poet is intoxicated by the beauty of nature and the harmony of life, it is moved to dance; and the expression of the dance is poetry. The difference between inspired poetry and mechanical writing is as great as the difference between true and false. For long ages the poets of

Persia have left a wonderful treasure of thought for humanity. Jelal-ud-Din Rumi has revealed in his *Masnavi* the mystery of profound revelation. In the East his works are considered as sacred as holy scriptures. They have illuminated numberless souls and the study of his work can be considered to belong to the highest standard of culture.

The poet is a creator, and he creates in spite of all that confronts him; he creates a world of his own. And by doing so he rises naturally above that plane where only what is visible and touchable is regarded as real. When he sings to the sun, when he smiles to the moon, when he prays to the sea, and when he looks at the plants, at the forests, and at life in the desert, he communicates with nature. In the eyes of the ordinary person he is imaginative, dreamy, visionary; his thoughts seem to be in the air. But if one asked the poet what he thinks of these others, he would say that it is those who cannot fly who remain on the ground. It is natural that creatures which walk on the earth are not always able to fly; those which fly in the air must have wings, and among human beings one will find that same difference, for in human beings there are all things.

There are souls like germs and worms, there are souls like animals and birds, and there are souls like jinns and angels.

Among human beings all can be found: those who belong to the earth, those who dwell in heaven, and those who dwell in the very depths.

Those who were able to soar upward by the power of their imagination have been living poets. What they said was not only a statement, it was music itself; it not only had a rhythm, but it had also a tone in it. It made their souls dance and it would make anyone dance who heard their poetry. Thus Hafiz of Shiraz gives a challenge to the dignified, pious men of his country when he says, 'Pious friends, you would forget your dignity if you would hear the song which came from my glowing heart.' And it is such souls who have touched the highest summits of life, so that they have been able to contribute some truth, giving an interpretation of human nature and the inner law of life.

It is another thing with poets who have made poetry for the sake of fame or name or popularity, or so that it might be appreciated by others; for that is business and not poetry. Poetry is an art, an art of the highest degree. The poet's communication with nature brings him in the end to communicate with himself, and by that communication he delves deeper and deeper, within and without, communicating with life everywhere. This communication brings him into a state of ecstasy, and in his ecstasy his whole being is filled with joy; he forgets the worries and anxieties of life, he rises above the praise and blame of this earth, and the things of this world become of less importance to him. He stands on the earth but gazes into the heavens; his outlook on life becomes broadened and his sight keen. He sees things that no one else is interested in, that no one else sees.

This teaches us that what may be called heaven or paradise is not very far from man. It is always near him, if only he would look at it. Our life is what we look at. If we look at the right thing then it is right; if we look at the wrong thing then it is wrong. Our life made according to our own attitude, and that is why the poet proves to be self-sufficient, and also indifferent and independent; these qualities become wings, for him to fly upward. The poet is in the same position as anyone else in regard to the fears and worries that life brings, the troubles and difficulties that everyone feels in the midst of the world, and yet he rises above these things so that they do not touch him.

No doubt the poet is much more sensitive to the troubles and difficulties of life than an ordinary person. If he took to heart everything that came to him, all the jarring influences that disturbed his peace of mind, all the rough edges of life that everyone has to rub against, he would not be able to go on; but on the other hand if he hardened his heart and made it less sensitive, then he would also close his heart to the inspiration which comes as poetry. Therefore in order to open the doors of his heart, to keep its sensitiveness, the one who communicates with life within and without is open to all influences whether agreeable or disagreeable and is without any protection; and his only escape from all the disturbances of life is through rising above them.

The prophetic message which was given by Zarathushtra (Zoroaster) to the people of Persia was poetic from beginning to end. It is most interesting to see that Zarathushtra showed in his scriptures and all through his life how a poet rises from earth to heaven. It suggests to us how Zarathushtra communicated with nature, with its beauty, and how at every step he took he touched deeper and deeper the depths of life. Zarathushtra formed his religion by praising the beauty in nature and by finding the source of his art which is creation itself in the Artist who is behind it all.

What form of worship did he teach? He taught the same worship with which he began his poetry and with which he finished it. He said to his pupils, 'Stand before the sea, look at the vastness of it, bow before it, before its source and goal.' He said to them, 'Look at the sun, and see what joy it brings. What is at the back of it? Where does it come from? Think of its source and goal, and how you are heading towards it.' People then thought that it was sun-worship, but it was not; it was the worship of light which is the source and goal of all. That communication within and without sometimes extended the range of a poet's vision so much that it was beyond the comprehension of the average man.

When the Shah of Persia said that he would like to have the history of his country written, for one did not exist at that time, Firdausi, a poet who was inspired and intuitive said, 'I will write it and bring it to you.' He began to meditate, throwing his searchlight as far back into the past as possible, and before the appointed time he was able to prepare that book and bring it to the court. It is said that the spiritual power of that poet was so great that when someone at the court sneered at the idea of a man being able to look so far back into the past, he went up to him and put his hand on his forehead and said, 'Now see!' And the man saw with his own eyes that which was written in the book.

This is human; it is not superhuman, although examples of it are rarely to be found; for in the life of every human being, especially of one who is pure-hearted, loving, sympathetic, and good, the past, present, and future are manifested to a certain extent. If one's inner light were thrown back as a searchlight it could go much further than man can comprehend. Some have it to develop this gift, but others are born with it; and among those who are born with it we find some who perhaps know ten or twelve years before and what is going to happen. Therefore a poet is someone who can focus his soul on the past, and also throw his light on the future, and make that clear which has not yet happened but which has been planned beforehand and which already exists in the abstract.

It is such poetry that becomes inspirational poetry. It is through such poetry that the intricate aspects of metaphysics can be taught. All the Upanishads of the Vedas are written in poetry; the suras of the Qu'ran and Zarathushtra's scriptures are all in poetry. All these prophets, whenever they came, brought the message in poetry.

The development of poetry in Persia occurred at a time when there was a great conflict between the orthodox and the freethinkers. At that time the law of the nation was a religious law and no one was at liberty to express his free thoughts which might be in conflict with the religious ideas.

And there were great thinkers such as Firdausi, Farid-al-din 'Attar, Jelal-ud-Din Rumi, Sa'di, Hafiz, Jami, Omar Khayyam, who were not only poets, but who were poetry itself. They were living in another world although they appeared to be on earth. Their outlook on life, their keen sight, were different to those of everyone else. The words which arose from their hearts were not brought forth with effort, they were natural flames rising up out of the heart. And these words remain as flames enlightening souls of all times, whatever soul they have touched.

Sufism has been the wisdom of these poets. There has never been a poet of note in Persia who was not a Sufi, and every one of them has added a certain aspect to the Sufi ideas, but they took great care not to affront the minds of orthodox people. Therefore a new terminology had to be invented in Persian poetry; the poets had to use words such as 'wine' and 'bowl' and 'beloved' and 'rose', words which would not offend the orthodox mind and would yet at the same time serve as symbolical expressions to explain the divine law." (All in brackets, by Paul Smith).

Further Reading...

The Sufi Message of Hazrat Inayat Khan Volume X: Sufi Mysticism; The Path of Initiation and Discipleship; **Sufi Poetry,** *Art: Yesterday, Today and Tomorrow; The Problem of the Day. Barrie and Jenkins, London, 1964. (Pages 119-154... after the three essays printed above Hazrat Inayat Khan goes on to talk about 'Attar, Rumi, Sadi and Hafiz).*

A History of Ottoman Poetry by E.J.W. Gibb. Volume One, Luzac & Co. Ltd. London 1900. (Pages 33-69.)

A Critical Appreciation of Arabic Mystical Poetry by Dr. S.H. Nadeem, Adam Publishers. New Delhi, 2003.

Sufi Poems, A Medieval Anthology by Martin Lings, Islamic Texts Society, Cambridge, 2004.

The Way of the Mystics: The Early Christian Mystics and The Rise of the Sufis by Margaret Smith, Sheldon Press, 1976.

In the Garden of Myrtles: Studies in Early Islamic Mysticism by Tor Andrae, Translated by Birgitta Sharpe. State University of New York Press, Albany. 1987.

Muslim Saints and Mystics... Episodes from the 'Memorial of the Saints' by Farid al-Din Attar, Translated by A.J. Arberry. Routledge and Kegan Paul, London, 1966.

Kashf Al-Mahjub of Al-Hujwiri. Translated by R.A. Nicholson, Luzac, London. 1967.

The Doctrine of the Sufis by Abu Bakr al-Kalabadhi, Translated by A.J. Arberry, Cambridge University Press 1935.

The Mystics of Islam by Reynold A. Nicholson. Routledge and Kegan Paul, London, reprint 1974.

The Idea of Personality in Sufism by Reynold Alleyne Nicholson, First Published 1923.

The Heritage of Sufism Volume One... Edited by Leonard Lewisohn, Oneworld Publications, Oxford, 1999.

Persian Mysticism by R.P. Masani, Award Publishing House, New Delhi, 1981.

Sufi Literature and the Journey to Immortality by A.E.I. Falconar, Motilal Banarsidass Publishers, Delhi, 1991.

An Introduction to Sufi Doctrine by Titus Burkhardt, Trans. by D.M. Matheson. Sh. Muhammad Ashraf, Lahore, 1973.

Persian Sufi Poetry: An Introduction to the Mystical Use of Classical Poems by J.T.P. De Bruijn. Curzon Press, 1997.

The Drunken Universe: An Anthology of Persian Sufi Poetry, Translation and Commentary by Peter Lamborn Wilson and Nasrollah Pourjavady. Phanes Press, Grand Rapids, 1987.

The Persian Sufis by Cyprian Rice, O.P. George Allen and Unwin Ltd, London, 1964.

God Speaks: The Theme of Creation and Its Purpose by Meher Baba. Dodd, Mead & Company, New York, 1955. (Meher Baba in great detail explains the Involution of the Soul and the seven stages of the Spiritual Path, the role of the Perfect Master, the Creation and the different States of God using quotations from Sufi poets and Masters and Sufi terminology and cross-referencing with Christian Mystical and Vedantic terminology. Meher Baba also quotes various couplets by Hafiz when describing the passage through the inner planes of consciousness to God-Realization).

The Hebraic Tongue Restored By Fabre d'Olivet. English Trans. by Nayan Louise Redfield. G.P. Putnam's & Sons. N.Y. 1921 (Fabre D'Olivet reconstructed ancient Hebrew and then faithfully translated Genesis... by using the Adamic Alphabet and revealed that its sounds really told the Divine love-story between Adam and Eve... in a spiral, also the form of the ghazal. See also my book and filmscript on Fabre D'Olivet and his miraculous powers of healing deaf mutes by blowing into their ears the original creative sound of original Adamic vowels... *The Healer and the Emperor*).

Some of the Poetic Forms Used by Zauq

The Ruba'i

Many scholars of Persian Poetry believe that the *ruba'i* is the most ancient Persian poetic form that is original to this language and they state that all other classical forms including the *ghazal, qasida, masnavi, qit'a* and others originated in Arabic literature and the metres employed in them were in Arabic poetry in the beginning... this, can be disputed.

The Persian language is a fine intercourse of Arabic (a masculine-sounding language) and Pahlavi (feminine-sounding language) that is mainly a descendant of the profound language of the Spiritual Master Zoroaster... Zend. Sanskrit is also a branch of that ancient language* (e.g. Zend: *garema* or heat is in Sanskrit *gharma,* in Pahlavi is *garma,* Persian... *garm)* given to us by that prophet whose perfect and profound teachings in the *gathas* of the *Avesta* were composed in a form very close to the *ruba'i* which one might believe could give him the title not only of the founder of the Persian language and people and mysticism... but also of Persian poetry's most individualistic form of poetic expression.

One can trace the origins of this poetical language back almost 7000 years to Zoroaster's time, not merely less than 2600 years... a mistake that most recent scholars made by confusing the last Zoroastian *priest* bearing his name with that of this original Prophet, the *Rasool* or Messiah, who like Moses, led out his people from their original Aryan lands in Bactria, when they were invaded by many hordes of murderous barbarians.

On that remarkable and in many aspects, far-reaching journey, an argument occurred amongst his people when they had reached what we today call India and many left him and settled there and their language eventually evolved into Sanskrit. Zoroaster then took his remaining followers west and finally settled near Shiraz in Fars, and Zend eventually became Pahlavi and the Aryan language continued west and founded many languages in Europe, including English.

Now as to the origin of the metre of the *ruba'i* I offer two of Zoroaster's poems or *gathas* to enjoy and consider, even though the metre may not be that of the *ruba'i*, the rhyme structure and content are similar.

Wise One, with these short poems I come before You,

praising Your Righteousness, deeds of Good Mind too.

And when I arrive at that bliss that has come to me...

may these poems of this man of insight... come through.

The *ruba'i* is a poem of four lines in which usually the first, second and fourth lines rhyme and sometimes with the *radif* (refrain) after the rhyme words... sometimes all four rhyme. It is composed in metres called *ruba'i* metres. Each *ruba'i* is a separate poem in itself and should not be regarded as a part of a long poem as was created by FitzGerald when he translated those he attributed to Omar Khayyam.

The *ruba'i* (as its name implies) is two couplets *(beyts)* in length, or four lines *(misra)*. The *ruba'i* is a different metre from those used in Arabic poetry that preceded it.

How was this metre invented? The accepted story of Rudaki (d. 941) creating this new *metre* of the *hazaj* group which is essential to the *ruba'i* is as follows: one New Year's Festival *(Nowruz)* he happened to be strolling in a garden where some children played with nuts and one threw a walnut along a groove in a stick and it jumped out then rolled back again creating a sound and the children shouted with delight in imitation, *'Ghaltan ghaltan hami ravad ta bun-i gau,'* *(Ball, ball, surprising hills to end of a brave try)*. Rudaki immediately recognised in the line's metre a new invention and by the repetition four times of the *rhyme* he had quickly created the *ruba'i*... and is considered the first master of this form and the father of classical Persian Poetry.

Shams-e Qais writing two hundred years later about this moment of poetic history and the effect of this new form on the population said the following... "This new poetic form fascinated all classes, rich and poor, ascetic and drunken rebel-outsider *[rend]*, all wanted to participate in it... the sinful and the good both loved it; those who were so ignorant they couldn't make out the difference between poetry and prose began to dance to it; those with dead hearts who couldn't tell the difference between a donkey braying and reed's wailing and were a thousand miles away from listening to a lute's strumming, offered up their souls for a *ruba'i*. Many young cloistered girls, from passion for the song of a *ruba'i* broke down the doors and their chastity's walls; many matrons from love for a *ruba'i* let loose the braids of their self-restraint."

And so, the *ruba'i* should be eloquent, spontaneous and ingenious. In the *ruba'i* the first three lines serve as an introduction to the fourth that should be sublime, subtle or pithy and clever. As can be seen from the quote by Shams-e Qais above, the *ruba'i* immediately appealed to all levels of society and has done so ever since. The nobility and royalty enjoyed those in praise of them and the commoner enjoyed the short, simple homilies... the ascetic and mystic could think upon epigrams of deep religious fervour and wisdom; the reprobates enjoyed the subtle and amusing satires and obscenities... and for everyone, especially the cloistered girls and old maids, many erotic and beautiful love poems to satisfy any passionate heart.

Almost every major and minor poet in Persia composed at some time in the *ruba'i* form.

Note: See 'Comparative Grammar, Lecture 6' in 'Lectures on the Science of Language' 1861 By Max Muller, Reprint Munshi Ram Manohar Lal, Delhi, 1965.
The Encyclopaedia Britannica Volume xxi, Eleventh Edition Cambridge 1911 (Pages 246-8).

The Ghazal.

There is really no equivalent to the *ghazal* (pronounced *guz'el*) in English poetry although Masud Farzaad,* perhaps the greatest Iranian authority on Hafiz (he spent much his lifetime finding the Variorum Edition) and his *ghazals* says, the sonnet is probably the closest. As a matter of fact, the *ghazal* is a unique form and its origin has been argued about for many centuries.

Some say that the *ghazal* originated in songs that were composed in Persia to be sung at court before Persia was converted to Islam, but not one song has survived to prove this. It is also possible that originally the *ghazals* were songs of love that were sung by minstrels in the early days of Persian history and that this form passed into poetry down the ages. I find this explanation plausible for the following reasons: firstly, the word *ghazal* means 'a conversation between lovers.' Secondly, the *ghazals* of Hafiz, Sadi and others were often put to music and became songs, which have been popular in Persia from ancient times until now.

Other scholars see the *ghazal* as coming from Arabic poetry, especially the prelude to longer poems: they say that this prelude was isolated and changed, to eventually become the *ghazal*. The Arabic root of the word *ghazal* is *gazl* which means: spinning, spun, thread, twist… the form of the *ghazal* is a spiral.

Whatever the origin, by the fourteenth century the *ghazal* had become a mature form of poetry. Among the great *ghazal* writers in Persian of the past were Nizami, Farid ad-Din 'Attar, Rumi and Sadi; but with the *ghazals* of Hafiz and other poets in Shiraz during his lifetime and those of Amir Khusrau this form reached its summit.

The form of the *ghazal* at first glance seems simple, but on a deeper inspection it will be found that there is more to it than one at first sees.

It is usually between five and fifteen couplets (*beyts* or 'houses'), but sometimes more. A *beyt* is 'a line of verse split into two equal parts scanning exactly alike.' Each couplet has a fixed rhyme that appears at the end of the second line. In the first couplet that is called the *matla* meaning 'orient' or 'rising,' the rhyme appears at the end of both lines. This first couplet has the function of 'setting the stage' or stating the subject matter and feeling of the poem. The other couplets or *beyts* have other names depending on their positions. One could say that the opening couplet is the subject, the following couplets the actions: changing, viewed from different angles, progressing from one point to another, larger and deeper, until the objective of the poem is reached in the last couplet. The final couplet is known as the *maqta* or 'point of section.' This couplet or the one before it almost always contains the *takhallus* or pen-name of the poet, signifying that it was written by him and also allowing him the chance to detach himself from himself and comment on what effect the actions of the subject matter in the preceding couplets had on him. Often the poet uses a play on words when he uses his own pen-name... ('Hafiz' for example, means: a preserver, a guardian, rememberer, watchman, one who knows the *Koran* by heart. 'Nizami' means: paradise).

In the *ghazal* the Persian Master Poets found the ideal instrument to express the great tension between the opposites that exist in this world. Having the strict rhyming structure of the same rhyme at the end of the second line of each couplet (after the first couplet) the mind must continually come back to the world and the poem and the rhyme. But by being allowed to use any word at the end of the first line of each couplet, one can be as spontaneous as possible and give the heart its full rein. This of course happens also in the first line of the first couplet, for whatever word or rhyme-sound that comes out in the first line sets the rhyme for the rest of the *ghazal*. So the 'feeling' created by the rhyme is one that comes spontaneously from the heart, and this spontaneity is allowed to be expanded from then on in the non-rhyming lines, and to contract in those lines that rhyme, when the mind must function as an 'orderer' of the poem. This expansion and contraction, feeling and thinking, heart and mind, combine to produce great tension and power that spirals inward and outward and creates an atmosphere that I would define as 'deep nostalgia.' This deep nostalgia is a primal moving force that flows through all life, art and song, and produces within whoever comes into contact with it when it is consciously expressed, an irresistible yearning to unite the opposites that it contains. In the *ghazal* any metre can be employed except the *ruba'i* metre.

The true meaning of Sufism, apart from the recognition of God in human form as the *Qutub* or the *Rasool* or the Christ is *tassawuf...* that means to get to the essence of everything. Adam was the first poet and it is said that he named everything and invented the first alphabet from which all others come. But Adam was not only the creator of conscious language as we know it, he was also the creator of song and the perfect form through which he created songs in praise of Eve his true Beloved, her beauty was displayed in the spiral form of the *ghazal.* So, the *ghazals* he composed and sung to her before their eventual Spiritual Union were of longing and separation and those after... of the bliss of Union. He used the same form of song about other events including the great sorrow and deep nostalgia about the loss of his favourite son Abel.

Two of Arabia's most careful and serious historians Tabari (d.923) and Masudi (d.957) state that the first poem ever composed in known history was one by Adam on the death of Abel and the form was the *ghazal*.

Although the poets of the *ghazal* may appear to many as open-minded, drunken, outcast lovers, it does not necessarily mean that they all drank the juice of the grape... for it is an inner state that they often were expressing. The *ghazal* is a conversation between the lover and the beloved and as in all intimate conversation... the talk flows both ways. The subject may not necessary be about love, but it is always from the point of view of one who loves truth, love and beauty.

Hafeez and his Poems by Masud Farzaad. Stephen Austin & Sons Ltd. Hertford, 1949.

The Qasida

This kind of poem resembles a *ghazal* in many ways except that it is longer than the *ghazal* and is often as long as a hundred couplets. In the first couplet, both the lines rhyme, and the same rhyme runs through the whole poem, the rhyme-word being at the end of the second line of each couplet (after the first couplet) as in the *ghazal*. The *qasida* (which means 'purpose') is usually written in praise of someone and is often read in his or her presence, so it is stated that it shouldn't be too long or it might weary the listener. It has a number of sections: i. *matla* - the beginning, ii. *taghazzul* -introduction, iii. *guriz* - the couplets in praise of whoever it is written to, iv. *maqta*- the end. In the *qasida,* the *takhallus* or pen-name of the poet usually does not appear, and if it does it is not necessarily near the end or at the end as in the *ghazal*. Any metre may be used except that used for the *ruba'i*.

The Qit'a

The *qit'a* or 'fragment' must consist of at least two couplets and is similar to a *ghazal* or a *qasida* with the second lines of the couplets all having the same rhyme... but in the first couplet the double-rhyme does not usually appear. It can be composed in any metre except for that of the *ruba'i*. It can be a fragment from a *qasida* or a *ghazal,* or it may be complete in itself. Hafiz and others often used this form to write obituaries on people whom he knew as did many other poets.

49

Ghazals...

I looked for Him everywhere, but Him I wasn't finding:

if I'd found Him not a trace of myself I'd be discovering.

When I discovered a man who was not the world's dog…

I found that an angel to that One, one can't be comparing.

If it was that all loss and gain only happens due to Fate,

nothing here was gained by us and we didn't lose a thing.

How is it possible, for this wound in my heart to speak?

It has been given a mouth, but no lips have it for speaking!

At times You were in it, at other times longing for You…

in other words, this mad heart empty I was never finding.

In this Universe where is one to match that One, Zauq?

One won't find that one; that One, one's not discovering!

Cruel one, if you killed a helpless one, what really did you

do?

If you killed one dying anyway, nothing brave was done by

you.

If self you didn't kill, when dust philosopher's stone exposes

turning ashes to mercury... it is a worthless thing you

do.

If you kill a lion, snake or a crocodile, it is no great wonder...

but if you kill desires and lust something good is done by

you.

Arrows of your sighs should've hit the evil eye or evil heart:

O Zauq, it was a useless thing to aim at a sky that's only

blue!

Laughter in world full of tears, gurgle of wine from a flask,

if one laughs and the sound travels far, no heart breaks in

two!

Who is the one who in Your gathering, mentioned

is not?

It is I who is never mentioned, my name ever said,

is not!

O heart, not justified is your complaint of being ignored:

tell me what you'll do, if sound of that one's tread,

is not.

If You plan to come make it soon, for little time remains:

let's see if my breath comes back, or it, if I'm dead,

is not!

Nonexistence should be more comfortable than existence:

that one who leaves here, returning let it be said:

"Is not!"

Time of death comes, at moment of longing to see You…

but, one word of longing through these lips said…

is not.

I'm only powerless before Fate, Zauq, or… it'd be that in

every art none equal me: what I don't know… read,

is not!

We are brought here by life, death tells us when to go…

who knows when we come, when we go who does know?

If we even had Khizer's lifetime we would still complain:

"In a short while we must go, we came not so long ago!"*

In this game that is called 'life' we're such a poor player:

every move of mine in this show wasn't a yes… but a no!

If the world doesn't interest our heart and soul it is good:

what to I do if I am not in it, I can't help this show to go!

Don't underestimate one's virtues, for Fate is too strong:

one's knowledge and wisdom… must to Fate finally bow.

Is there a soul on the earth the world faithful to has been?

Best to travel along time's tide, with its ebb and flow go!

On wings of love we're leaving this meadow here, Zauq,

what do we care if morning breeze doesn't, or does blow?

---

*Note: Khizer is often called: "The Green One" for he was said to have drunk
from the Fountain of Immortality and gained Eternal life. He has been
identified with Elias, St. George, Phineas, the Angel Gabriel, the companion
of Mohammed on a journey which is told in the Koran, viii, 59-81, and
throughout the literature of Mysticism has appeared to many great seekers
who eventually became Perfect Masters. See my 'Khidr in Sufi Poetry' New
Humanity Books, 2012.

I'm fearful today that I'll not be surviving…

won't come:

unless Messiah-like One of mine is arriving,

won't come.

Your meeting at night with others all are talking of:

no, only to me this privilege You're denying"

"Won't come!"

Although my breath's choked up by my deep desire,

word of what I want to my lips isn't coming:

won't come!

O heart it's futile to complain that One won't come!

O sir, tell me what you'd do if that Darling…

won't come?

Destiny has forced me down, O Zauq: if not so with

all of my skills I still don't know, that arriving

won't come!

Grasping the heartsick heart of the lover, You're

going...

to take the fire You had come, now away, forever

going?

See how that proud beauty doesn't want to walk the earth;

strutting in space like the sun, all the time clever,

going!

In Your street we received, what? Like a morning breeze in

dust blown about, our way back we are again there

going!

The sight of the sick eye cannot be restored by collyrium...

see how virtuous leave the world, with slate cleaner

going.

We are coming into this world riding upon a winged horse:

not allowed to stay, what a way to come... be later

going!

Listen, peace upon this earth... when have they found it:

the people who by lust and greed are more and more

going?

O Zauq, what a fatal thing is that one's deadly glance!

Who can save one when such a deadly dart is here

going?

Though from woe we say we'll make this life's ending

be:

we'll do what if from death, no relief from suffering…

be?

If that home of that rival to visit you have thought about;

like us, such plans as that, one should now revising

be!

Listen, I'm not that type who would sue one for murder…

I'd deny everything, even if I by God interrogating

be!

Even all of the fires of hell will be shivering out of shame,

when all us sinners in guilt soaked, in hell arriving

be!

No print and no image and no sign we'll leave behind…

like that shooting glance, us from here shall flying

be!

Zauq, that school in the mosque has spoilt the *mulla*…

bring to this Winehouse, that one us will saving

be!

We come, brought here by life, by death we are to
go…

not from our will we come, not from it we it's true
go.

We'll complain, even if like Khizer we're given eternal life:
"We came here awhile ago and in another we too,
go!"

And in this field of life I continue to be such a poor player:
each move that I am making is a poor show… to,
go!

If heart and soul of ours the world doesn't move it is good:
we can do what? Unless involved, never in it... do
go!

Fate is much too tough so don't brag of all your virtues…
humour of yours and wisdom of mine, do the two
go?

To any upon this earth has this world ever shown faith?
Along tide of time as it ebbs and flows, now, you
go.

On wings of love carried, we leave this grove, O Zauq:
why worry whether a morning breeze may through
go?

Being in love can be cruel, full of fighting,

it's so...

the lover must with fate go on wrestling,

it's so!

Fires flare up for no reason where so many gather:

candle burns without any breeze blowing;

it's so!

Destiny with beauties is like battle with the self:

see how the fool for God keeps on looking:

it's so!

The gurgling sound of this daughter of the vine...

why does it a virtuous person be bothering,

it's so?

No eyelashes have lines to speak so eloquently:

one calamity after another, is happening...

it's so!

That glance of love on the lover can be likened to

contamination that goes on contaminating:

it's so!

Your ailing patient that is out upon this terrace

knows only of death, death with no healing,

it's so.

This old world has no peace on any given day...

all these quarrelsome ones keep quarreling,

it's so.

Praise be given to all the followers of the Self:

love begins inside of us, the real beginning;

it's so!

See those intoxicating eyes, full of mischief...

after some one who their self is restraining:

it's so!

Your bloody sword goes on splashing again...

all those stains, water of life is bestowing,

it's so.

Is truth just an illusion, a strategy, O Zauq?

Glance can only deceit, fraud be offering...

it's so?

O Zauq, time of complaints testing heart's bravery,

on hand…

or heart will cry out to You to conquer the difficulty

on hand.

Heart didn't leave, was patient, not relieved nor tranquil:

Your glance was not clear, but made home, homely,

on hand.

These pleasures eaten like the sorrows of love of my heart:

like one famished, devouring *halva* O so greedily…

on hand.

Give a letter of needs, or by word of mouth, a few words:

however, keep heart in letter someone is carrying…

by hand.

Five branches You haven't burnt, my fingers, O Doctor!

I'll retain that warmth, ardour, lover's anguishing,

on hand.

With all this killing, tyranny, it's get up, not in awhile…

be at tomb of one killed by glance, sword thrusting:

on hand!

I'm so feeble; I'm worthless dust of a lover, dust storm…

I'll get up, I will shoulder the of breeze of morning,

on hand.

O candle, one Thief it is behind this morning breeze...
one each breath, with Your gold crown it's hitting
on hand!
O Zauq, I'll then sit on straw of soul to hold it to task:
gift of grace will stay as They the waist are circling
on hand.

You're not coming home again, I don't know how to

listen...

hear me; stay or go, no how or why, to this then you

listen!

Listen to the stories of Majnun and Farhad, my friend...*

while hearing the tales we lost our self, so you to...

listen!

Complaints were made about us; no abuse today arrives:

many a reproach that arrived, to not even that too

listen.

Some say to stay, advising on what they do not know...

giving nothing away I then, "Get drunk enough to

listen!"

Don't say how it started, that's the truth to tell on day:

sometimes telling half, sometime to half... will you

listen?

The face will reveal the self to see, as the form too does:

the voice also is the same to who need to know too!

Listen!

Price in heart's wares on order for Zauq to get one kiss

is what, is what, not that, not together be pure to

listen?

*Notes: Majnun (about 721 A.D.) which means 'madman' whose real name was Qays, was the famous lover of Layla who came from another tribe in Arabia. Majnun fell in love with Layla when they were children at school together. Unable to contain his love, one day he expressed it and Layla's father, enraged by the scandal of this 'madman' in love with his daughter, refused to allow them to see etch other. Majnun's father, who was the leader of his tribe, tried to reconcile them but to no avail. Layla also loved Majnun. Majnun wandered the hills living with wild animals and composing songs in praise of Layla. Finally their human love became so great that it was transformed into Divine Love by a Perfect Master. Layla became so undernourished from missing him that she finally starved to death. Majnun threw himself on her grave and died there. Their souls mingled with their dust. Many stories and poems have been written about them, the most popular being that by Nizami.... See my translation of his version, New Humanity Books, 2012 and his own poems, 'Poems of Majnun', New Humanity Books, 2012.

*Shirin was said to be the beautiful daughter of the Byzantine Emperor, Maurice. She married Parviz (A.D.591) and became the queen of Persia. It was Parviz who invaded Jerusalem and carried away the true cross. A sculptor by the name of Farhad fell in love with her and she with him. Farhad made an agreement with Parviz that if he could cut a pass through a mountain with his axe for a water-channel, he would be given Shirin. After many years he achieved this remarkable feat (it still exists today) but on hearing that he had succeeded Parviz sent a messenger to tell him that Shirin had committed suicide. On hearing this lie, Farhad threw himself off the mountain and died. This tragic love story is very popular in Persian legend and poetry especially in the masnavis of Nizami and Amir Khusrau.

Now, the fear that soon that we will be dead,

will pass...

but dead now is all peace, no doubt it's said...

will pass.

You don't decide who is the rival that sets up home here:

desires here are few, even another homestead

will pass.

O healers, empty are those cures in your ointment boxes:

bruises on me, unseen throughout this world...

will pass.

We'll reach to way of Beloved, then we will be as one...

first we'll not look worldly situation, that road

will pass.

Flame of sigh becomes lightning growing even brighter:

but I am not afraid that what I see, it I feared,

will pass.

We are not with those killers claiming to work for You:

on the contrary, ask God; that which is denied

will pass.

Hell's fire in the belly, also it will pass. Water! Water!

When a sinner sweats from shame... saturated,

will pass!

No one will ever discover another like us, no, not ever!

in world we're all for glance's arrow that inward

will pass.

In presence of the tearful eyes speaking out like a river;

we ascend, if we rise to glance, that downward

will pass.

Bring the drunkard, yes, a tomb... that of the rosy eyes:

but, if another few, not flowers, then I instead,

will pass.

The bright face from veil lifted so now we can see You:

look on the sun and moon for friends soon dead

will pass.

As one we too will see the people of insight, or won't:

here, while we seek glance's arrow that inward

will pass.

Zauq, whose school of Islam's spoiled due to *mullahs*,

is off to the winehouse inside to get intoxicated!

Will pass?

Dear ones, this is not the gong that is sounding:

understand…

these past lives we can now hear away running…

understand?

Appropriate words say of world, appropriate speaking,

understand:

voice of the people about wish of God be telling…

understand?

Don't understand forest, or clinic for insane, the both:

that worthless dust also rests, eaten, foe curing…

understand?

Your judgement is tasteless, although learning is not:

judgement isn't blind with no stick for walking…

understand!

Write a book of stories of what to do to purify heart…

although Safa* of heart is from a grave, purifying,

understand?

Who laughs at me, then is crying through eyelashes?

I don't understand your wall built up of laughing.

Understand?

Desires that come and go are prayers of those alive:

but when they're dying, them they're neglecting;

understand?

Your road in meets dust of hundreds of thousands:

your desire is in your feet's dust that's blowing:

understand!

Saying prayers we do as killer's sword takes heart!

Lips that tear into the heart are lips for praying:

understand?

Value give me in blood, not of self, in inner lane...

that to friends, know for murder compensating,

understand.

Judgement is yours too; tell me you are satisfied...

your own heart with God goes so be listening:

understand?

Self calls your name in all you do, like a mirror...

who comes in person though by face knowing,

understand.

Fate's bowstring brings chaos, arrow of tyranny:

our collapse to you then is mere dust swirling:

understand?

Nothing is tiny, pure gold, face of saffron colour:

love your Self, O Zauq; alchemy transforming

understand.

*Note: Safa is the sacred well of pure water near the Kaaba
in Mecca.*

World's garden in the universe to an oasis of *henna*

is belonging…

a heart full of blood over there, on hand like a letter

is belonging.

Each thirsting, worried, wounded heart over there,

is belonging…

so when you jump it's within your breast, to care

is belonging.

Where heart plays to entertain, upon my share…

is belonging…

wherever heart sticks, like life it to beyond repair

is belonging!

What disasters from time falling on us, not to be fixed:

palm-tree in a hurricane ripped out; out from there

is belonging?

Attach heart to pleasure for it is a sweetmeat within:

all roasted meat, salted, is a heart that to turn over

is belonging!

No night of separation belongs, to be told by mouth!

No, another side of my bed to about even to care…

is belonging.

No beggar, the ointment of rust is thanks to You...

heart's cut is poisoned, my laugh to You forever

is belonging.

Dagger's sharpness that is poisonous water is true:

perhaps water of this country to the Destroyer,

is belonging!

Majnun's height one at first took a rod to, it is so:

a bit would bend those feet, but one to despair

is belonging.

O pale devotee, it is then all bad for heart within?

Zauq, on that gold as touchstone, tight finger

is belonging!

Calamities seen can be into a mind, permanently

taken...

all of us, hands, eyelashes, by desires are usually

taken.

All have seen curl of hair, a madness, debt to be

taken...

the real gain all see is really a trap, price, costly

taken!

Night of union of day of separation within, without:

my destiny lies before me, a retaliation terribly

taken!

The moon's scar of slavery is not only there at rest...

They value like this, thousands of slaves, to be

taken!

Such as us with the power to convince, it's all a test:

who loves in a troubled heart, is another lover...

taken.

Bubbling water sounds, not telling of the killer, You:

they ask of death; only one name, You the giver

taken.

Your captive, the hunted, it's so... to You now begs:

then after, a breath... then not, bait of Hunter

taken!

It's like a bow, head bowed obediently, a new moon:

the pride of beauty by what salutation on offer,

taken.

Your graceful walk for many followers is mischief…

some footsteps momentarily are in time, forever

taken!

My hand, by Zauq, has time to drink more wine…

thousand graces by who of wine are, a partaker,

taken!

Lightning in my shelter, long ago was burning...

what came, went...

some dusty, escaped the storm, then off flying...

(what came, went).

On the footsteps: until no fear if one's coming:

what came, went!

Ah, give life: candle gave then later was dying:

what came, went!

Weakness we have of arm and hand for lifting:

what came, went...

the ant's like the ant, the seed to be displacing:

what came, went!

Fresh face like dawn, then night's hair that sighed...

O heart, so much happened, disaster following,

what came, went?

Blood of Farhad, was at that skirt of the mountain...

why no river to get rid of lover's blood staining?

What came, went?

You never leave the fellow-travelers in the caravan:

but, sound of the camels bells are us awakening:

what came, went!

Your eyebrows point, chest wounded as we stood...

pieces of heart as bouquet we were transforming:

what came, went!

We saw heart that attracted Layla in that camel...

to Majnun at last the way was there beginning:

what came, went!

Hey, inflammation's in that lane of flighting, sighs...

at night we hear footsteps, they're all revealing:

what came, went.

They went home strangers; we breathed a breeze...

suspecting those at home, or to hoer returning:

what came, went!

Who is a lover who is In lane of Your place to stay

will tell of divine destiny that was uplifting...

what came, went.

Desert of frenzy, an inner whirlwind was madness

You gave: Majnun's soul, for the welcoming...

what came, went!

The inner flame is Who drops in to stay with lover:

that burning fire of love, it went on burning...

what came, went.

O houri, side up to me and say to all with a glance:

heart flies to take whatever to be attracting...

what came, went.

Zauq came to where, then of its self a place was not:

the street of lovers dying unjustly are staying...

what came, went?

Silently, silently, grief we're experiencing,

we all learn from this:

heart, in heart anger do not be expressing,

we all learn from this.

Tears from clouds, continue to be falling…

we all learn from this.

What is this lightning, anger expressing?

We all learn from this!

A perfect glow of beauty now be bringing:

we all learn from this…

from any still behind the curtain burning,

we all learn from this.

Unreal is what from opium we're having:

we all learn from this…

what is up a sleeve can be quite alarming,

we all learn from this.

Hear of a visit immediately over and now we go:

get a Guide to gain some understanding,

we all learn from this.

We're not first or only to say You will destroy us!

The method of understanding be reaching:

we all learn from this.

Enjoy, wake up, however it's accepted it is grace!

First comes that grace that up us is raising:

we all learn from this!

Who learns from fate is faithful to an outsider...

whatever is taught that one is us teaching:

we all learn from this.

See Killer bringing everywhere a bleeding heart...

the truth is it is best to just go on smiling:

we all learn from this.

Arrow and its tip in heart as a candle still is lit:

by our arm, home away we're squandering:

we all learn from this.

Tell the messenger with any excuse to get there:

if it does not happen then us be excusing...

we all learn from this.

In a letter write it; send off a verse of sympathy:

heart's sorrow we should be emphasizing:

we all learn from this.

When talking of death it's said the head hurts:

to lie or not be truthful can be revealing...

we all learn from this.

There, trembling eyebrow, here an embrace it is:

gossip giving advice, is what achieving...

we all learn from this?

A sword here is absurd; if it fell we'd let it rest:

heart to an assassin, is here to be taking:

we all learn from this.

Wound to stitch for needle, picker of diamonds:

a chest cut open that stitches is needing:

we all learn from this.

I asked *mulla* who bowed head low mistakenly:

learn in the event this one is forgetting...

we all learn from this.

It happened O Zauq, eye's pupil is black-faced:

but eyes within are still comprehending...

we all learn from this!

A river of tears from the eyes in a moment,

like dry grass flowing...

listen, take it in, sky is a great monument:

like dry grass flowing.

Sacrifices be on tenderness of love, so heart bleeds:

arrow and tip in a breast like yours is spent

like dry grass flowing.

Devotee, drink wine like an infidel, like I do also...

one and half handfuls of this our creed went

like dry grass flowing.

A wave of love's ocean protecting against storms:

us, a handful of dust... a mere human being

like dry grass flowing.

A river of tears at time of writing is heart's state...

my form is a boat, or, a pen case for writing

like dry grass flowing.

This weeping, bursting, breaking, blistering water,

are like out into wilderness shouting, crying,

like dry grass flowing!

You were valued too much, because of those lips?

Yours are valued, rubies on moon glittering,

like dry grass flowing.

Boat riding this age, on ocean of death, in Zauq...

moments of worth, like dry grass flowing,

like dry grass flowing!

Was Zauq first in Punjab's Delhi to see beauty?

Now, on water in Multan* the inscribing:

'Like dry grass flowing.'

*Note: Multan is another city in the Punjab, now in Pakistan,
its 5th most populous city. Four years after Zauq dies the 'siege of Multan'
by the British began.

Do not reveal that navel's mole, O one so graceful,

to me...

here, each bit of the tulip is of navel's musk full...

to me.

Friend's fault for calamity is not just a slight pull

to me...

I am suspecting a hateful one is being so hateful

to me.

Wanderer in flower garden is being mad, spiteful

to me...

chain of feet is wave of breeze in garden, helpful

to me.

At a round of prayers in assembly, one can see the Imam:

God is paymaster not an assembly, though full,

to me.

O jasmine, O You my one with the bright, white teeth...

garden in us is why we cry as jasmine's graceful

to me.

Archway is to *Kaaba* when it is the curve of Your bow...

hunted in shrine know You shoot an arrow, fateful

to 'me'.

It's new hair growing on the body of dry, withered bones:

why pull out a thorn that weakens body, it's painful

to me?

O coloured lips that toss away a cheap a blue sapphire,

O give ruby, give to one Yeman's ruby so colourful

to me!

O yes the candle's wax is telling us the night is gone...

although lamp's glass remains it is merely wasteful

to me.

In land of tulips blooming in autumn, it's soon decay...

it's the same new stain and an old wound unhelpful

to me.

Khusrau never used an axe but still spilled that blood:

Shirin's blood was not on Farhad's head; spiteful…

to me. *

Upon Your face is a price unseen and it is not green:

come and look, it's eye of mouth so rare, tasteful

to me.

This heart, it's to give to the land, sky, only ashes…

one moment of lightning gives a secret insightful

to me.

In a lane Your existence was attainable, great news!

No moonlit night wearing shroud, it's mournful

to me.

Heavens showed the face of the earth for recreation:

more beautiful than moon, Your forehead is full

to me.

Store up the eye's rewards on whom You flirt with…

give a winecup by winebringer who is untrustful

to me.

It's right heart feels much in the well of separation!

You'd pull back curl from ear; it's a line unhelpful

to me!

You revealed a loving move, a hundred more to do:

simple thing done innocently is one so truthful

to me.

In wells that are alike, a star, eye's pupil shines in:

heart sees it's in pit of chin's dimple, an eyeful

to me.

Ah, come do that and give eyes something to see:

the eyes reveal what remains; a gazelle, playful

to me.

O come to me in the garden so You feel a breeze:

heart's desert came to each garden; so painful

to me.

O Lord, my heart's missing mirror of perception:

reveal where, I will go to door, land; be helpful

to me!

Yes, light… bringing to poets' gathering Zauq:

eyes on me, I sit; will they be more insightful

to me?

*Farhad: Shirin was said to be the beautiful daughter of the Byzantine Emperor, Maurice. She married Khusrau Parviz (A.D.591) and became the queen of Persia. It was Khusrau who invaded Jerusalem and carried away the true cross. A sculptor by the name of Farhad fell in love with her and she with him. Farhad made an agreement with Khusrau that if he could cut a pass through a mountain with his axe for a water-channel, he would be given Shirin. After many years he achieved this remarkable feat (it still exists today) but on hearing that he had succeeded Khusrau sent a messenger to tell him that Shirin had committed suicide. On hearing this lie, Farhad threw himself off the mountain and died. This tragic love story is very popular in Persian legend and poetry especially in the masnavi of Nizami.

A blow to this grieving heart of mine by a friend,

it's so…

it's a hit from a friend in the guts to bring an end:

it's so!

It's small coin, a small coin, not the apocalypse to see:

it happened so long ago; some, it would extend:

it's so!

It's difficult to be love's martyr, to see all the daggers:

many thanks for fruit of oasis of the contented,

it's so.

I was a candle weeping for the new, agreeable things:

it moved into me at night, a disaster existed;

it's so!

It's a pain in the heart, no sympathiser to bring help:

moving one doesn't occur as heart is busted;

it's so!

O heart full of pain and grief, tight, distressed too…

cheerful though ruined, at home, inhabited:

it's so!

On grave of the bereaved not even a lamp or a rose:

within breast heart burns and liver's scarred;

it's so.

In that invisible inside tell, say it again… thanks!

Though silent like dry grass I'll see it to end:

it's so!

Boat in ocean of grief I'm the Truth, God's sword!

To give in to one breath this way, it to send:

it's so!

Hearts of all burning with love will not be, Zauq:

it's better to together try find what sparkled;

it's so!

Friends are gone as from meetings, as it is written:

at rest in heart and mind in You, hearts all within!

At times mix then remain apart, like eyelashes are:

show temperament; it's sincerity, powerful within.

Expect of life the disease of separation from You...

no motion in pulse in the angry, be grateful within.

Reveal the skill to sigh at authority to protect self:

then stop hand of doomsday, sky dreadful within.

Who is that ascetic thinking of drunken eyebrows?

See house of Beloved within, a Temple, all within!

Knowing lips say words of complaint of this time:

a breathless melancholy for You was full, within.

Breeze from Beloved's lane made us astonished...

in weak body a soul; form, hay a handful, within.

Though I'm form I promise I'll trust in only One:

thousands promised... words had to eat back in!

All happened for an objective Zauq, two books...

humans have senses five, as lines of verse within.

A mouth's a rose-bud to open and the story

be telling… it's so:

perhaps to see peace be on one to eventually

be telling… it's so!

Quality of eyes and lips of the Friend only

be telling: it's so

that today a lesson of hints, signs, openly

be telling. It's so,

today with a foe is a desire to talk, quickly

be telling… it's so:

there is no known way to all that we see…

be telling; it's so!

Ask of the murderer, the one long ago, the killing:

today is the day we die, O death finally

be telling it's so!

Hand in Yours, a sacrifice, O what killer arrows!

All mouths of wounds, facing openly…

be telling, it's so!

That funeral of Zauq in time came to be watched:

when permission's given my kin finally

be telling… it's so.

A riot by the zealous against life unendurable

now...

a wink, a smile's flash and sparks fall on all...

now!

I'm a martyr to Beloved's smiling lips so full,

now...

All this light, laughter, my tomb's lovable...

now.

Heart's secrets aren't friend's: Friend is all,

now...

hearts not veiled by dust, not uncomfortable

now!

On that bright face and upon on every distilled drop...

words like stars, it's dawn of spring, audible

now!

It is union within and eye's hope, that through door

will fly back like straw my Friend, so lovable

now!

You'll arrive like food of the dove before and after...

for love-letters from You impatient we're all

now.

Although sacred, pure, holy, the pain is a danger...

a glance through lashes is a thorn, it's hurtful

now!

Extinguish heart of fire but not by throwing dust...

the tree will become my coffin, made of maple

now.

See the ear's door near the cheek, almost touching;

don't look at star, dawn of spring isn't visible

now!

It is asked: "Why taste the bitter water of tears?"

it's sherbet in Paradise, pomegranate to pull

now!

A trick of heart by eyelashes of Beloved's eyes...

it's desire on the grass with a chase invisible,

now!

Messenger, write a letter to the dust from me...

I don't know words: it's to one poor, unable,

now!

Zauq, if sense returns it's a world off, good luck!

Inside this winehouse, no desire to be able...

now!

Ruba'is...

O Zauq, we are here to suffer grief's pain,

no one knows why we come, and go again.

Upon this world's stage we enter... crying,

and as we leave others will cry out in vain.

O Zauq, that this ignorance all limits defies,

is certain;

that with all our learning we're still not wise,

is certain.

That learning would our hearts enlighten we were told,

but, that "We know nothing," as our life dies,

is certain.

Why should one uselessly worry about gain or loss?

We "Did this, and that;" claiming we are the boss.

Without Your Divine Grace nothing was gained...

and nothing will unless in Your Name, 'The Boss!'

Cut love's thread, Zauq, it you to this world is

binding,

and allow this hair on its original head to be

uncurling.

O Zauq, I know that you will never be leaving this hag,

though this hag will one day in the lurch, you be

leaving.

To the *jinn* this time of Islam isn't one that is

completed:

reflection seen, then, O Zauq is of one being

obliterated!

Those that laughed gave up all to the non-believer:

mimicking Muslim is that impious one who

imitated!

With that killer my eyes have clashed…

it's so…

life is caught in a duel until one is dead,

it's so!

Knowing no peace is this old hag of a world…

fought and fought, on war it's been fed:

it's so!

Qit'as…

Yesterday... Your love-sick lover's friends were about sick heart, health worse, much concerned. But now tears in eyes, they're looking for coffin cloth, a place to bury, of course much concerned.

Eyes cry, "Heart has completely finished us,"

my heart cries, "Eyes me into the deep gave!"

In this tug-of-war Zauq has not lost a thing:

I cry of my fate, as they to me no sleep gave.

The gift of breath is given to the worldly-wise:

we should all praise Your workmanship,

it's so!

Speaking the truth is up to each one, O Zauq:

wealth of war survivor is with fate's help:

it's so!

You're good, then bad, though not, O Zauq!

It's bad that the one you're bad to knowing

is.

If one is only bad; it's, that one truth telling

is...

why be bad, say... bad, fine to be accepting

is!

You leave that winehouse like some thief, so guiltily:

hiding up your sleeve is the flask of wine,

it's so!

O Zauq, stop all of your claims of piety; stop it now!

loud praises of God don't sound so fine...

it's so!

At home, could one's talent survive... and thrive?

Why should a ruby of Badakhshan have to

go far?

Zauq, though in Deccan the Muse respect gets...

lanes of Delhi who would leave, would you

go far?

*Note: The ruby of Badakhshan is said to be the most perfect. It is lilac in color and known as the Balais ruby.

Qasida...

In the garden the cooling breeze is blowing...

like a strong man's pulse it is evenly flowing.

The breeze like Messiah's breath refreshes...

the shady trees in the glade are a cure giving.

Bruised, wounded roses are healed by dew...

the rain drops broken branches are soothing.

Breeze's touch of sorcery clears all madness

and unscarred tulip goes on... easily waving.

Breeze in this garden makes the blood flow...

the red glow of *henna* every leaf is absorbing.

In all fiery faces new blood surges through...

those white like a lily are now red... glowing.

Bitterness has left everything, gall has gone:
sweet as honey is poison... opium is healing.
On this earth's stage security and joy reign:
this grinding stone causes no more suffering.

Cataracts of eyes that are opaque like pearls
are freed to see the sight that it was covering.
World's health's so much better wise doctors
do not need new cures, for old ways of dying.

From all of the body pain wants to stay away
and even letters spelling 'ache' are separating.
Such a height is now gained by world's health
that all over a sense of peace all are breathing.

From this earth disease has gone so fast, that

no one could call narcissus sick, or... anything!

The health of this world we all can now enjoy,

for today recovering from sickness is the king!

Poets and minstrels are joyful from this news,

of their lord and king they are praises singing.

I'll also sing a song of praise and follow them,

and all nightingales should encores be giving.

On earth today a fortunate day has arrived…
phoenixes will be born if crows, eggs are laying.
From news that your health's back life is back:
dead will also come back, due to your healing!

Lord, your life to that of us all is connected...
your royal grace is life's fountain for drinking.
And when you are bathing the drops that fall
become precious pearls that we can be seeing.

If they're used to make a cure for this sad time

all bones that are brittle by it are rejuvenating!

When washing your body, the dirt all gone was

like world of bad times away you were washing.

And... the stony heart of your foe full of hatred,

under your footstool's kept, all spite restraining.

Breeze comes with soft petals from rose-garden,

heavy clouds drop pearls in greetings, blessing.

On your day of recovery, how to tell of all this?

World's a joyful abode, laughter is all infecting!

One can see everywhere, fine pictures painted...

dancers happily dancing, everywhere is dancing.

Strutting on the grass is not only the peacock...

stuck in nests all other birds, are also strutting.

Inside all our eyes all our eyeballs now dance...

as each youthful one's sport is now... dancing!

All fireworks are making patterns like flowers,

that stars in the heavens find it O so amazing.

In excited voices they praised the show… said

alchemists stone with powder we were mixing!

In any other way could we fire such high balls...

that could the iron dust into gold be changing?

Into the sky such dazzling stars flew that many

thought it a laughing beauty… teeth sparkling!

Such a banquet went on that in its sun-like face

Jamshid's famous parties all glitter were losing!

All power in my pen's drained, no more to write,

so Zauq, hands in the air, to God is appealing...

"O Doctor, bless my king with perfect health...

may all that one's enemies be always grieving!"

Sher (Rhyming Couplets)...

Are there roses of pleasure in world's

garden?

Yes there are, but for them I care not,

again!

Who seeks learning, not love, who isn't

mad,

that one may be Plato but is not friend I

had.

The earth's in motion as the heavens revolve

and for this one also... no rest does involve!

If at departure Friend pours water onto my dry

lips...

bitterness of death become sweetness at finger

tips!

House of my life adjoins the wood of non-

existence...

it is open to me, but I don't walk into it...

hence.

O Zauq, in this world of forms are a million

appearances…

all are creation of the Artist and no one is…

less.

Inside the revolving cosmos this life of

mine

passes as boat on a river that moves so

fine!

In this world, let your heart move on and

on…

don't keep still, for standing water emits

stagnation.

O Khizer,* tales of infinity of creation are

fictitious...

in this changing world is no stability for

us.

I'm testing quality of my heart in this
gathering;
then so… to whom, will it at first be
turning?

If my equanimity I recover I will be

giving

wealth, fame, but never my heart…

giving.

The sweetness of my song the singing birds

borrowed…

the cry of the nightingale, is lost in all that…

orchestrated.

A symbol of the harvest is every grain...

in each drop, a sea; in part, see creation!

Roses will grow and bloom from ashes of my

body…

for I've died in contemplation of the Friend

only.

Full of this love's wine and of this world

forgetfulness

I sit like wine-cup, but seal on lip, I can't

express!

Don't bathe my corpse, let dust of Friend's

street

that decorates it, now stay there forever... I

entreat!

O misery… love demands heart is fixed

on the letter in the place of… the sealed.

It doesn't matter if the wine-cup my lip

touches…

because this heart of mine upon 'Ali set

is!*

O Zauq, careful, don't let mouth touch juice of the

grape...

such an infidel if allowed to kiss your lip will never

escape!

A tiny worm can bore a hole in a stone, so of what

part

is a heart of one if it doesn't dig deep, into Friend's

heart?

If I weep I will make many rivers to be

flowing…

I'm not content to imitate the dew in

weeping.

O Zauq, if one leaves home respect one is

renouncing...

pearl taken from sea, from hand to hand is

selling!

O Zauq, do not be following the advice of

reason…

dictates of love are final, all else… further

on!

For the sake of heart's purity, don't let the dust of

separation

stop mirror's transparency... if it stays there it is

illusion.

To street of the Friend of unfading roses, I'm

going...

O court of Delhi, capital of Hindustan, I'm

leaving!

In the state of old age... it to me

seems

mistakes of youth are tales of...

dreams!

Even, if by chance, you do not remember
me...
in remembering you, I've forgotten all I
see!

Winebringer, take the jug and the cup from the

niche..

and then the *Koran* into that empty space do...

pitch.

I pass this life oblivious of the world...and of

me:

self-forgetfulness is higher than remembering

me!

Breeze of dawn brought rumour of rose's
blooming...
birds in traps flew to garden their traps
carrying!

O heart, don't betray inner secrets of love and

peace…

with your eyes see but with lips say nothing, no

piece!

I'm unconcerned with Islam or with any

infidelity...

as I gave heart to You I am of all creeds

free!

O Zauq, a stone is better than a heart

without

love, as a stone in it has a spark to get

out!

You talk about taking your life out of

fear...

what to do after death you face more,

dear?

O Zauq, be taking to the winehouse... to

reform,

those who in school are spoiled since being

born!

I'm not one who will charge You with killing

me...

if on Last Day God asks if You killed me...

negativity!

I was brought here by life, but... I go as death me is

calling:

I didn't come here due to me, I don't leave happily

going!

If even a thousand years I live at the hour of

passing

the time of my life will seem to be one spring

morning!

Knitting brows, You may stone me with a thousand
abuses...
it will never be disturbing the peace of my love... no
excuses!

O candle, the span of your life is only one

night…

it is for you to pass it in tears or in smiles,

tonight!

For all stars in heaven lover wouldn't exchange

teardrops…

for who would take empty shells in return for

pearl-drops?

O you, learn the spirit of chivalry from the

mosquito…

before it takes its blood it warns its victims

so!

When fate caused a thousand wounds on you no
complaint
escaped your lips… O well done, O Zauq, do not
faint!

Don't ask me whether my heart is in joy or

woe…

O friend I'm oblivious of both, so on I now

go!

Under all circumstances in this world with truth

stay...

Zauq, it's a sword in youth, in old age a staff, I

say.

As I left the world despair whispered on my death-
bed…
"Don't go by yourself, I will be with you." This, I
dread!

If the delights of dying lovers could tell...
Jesus would wish to die of love as well.

If the roses knew they'd be chosen, and

picked...

they would never wish for colour and be

scented!

I'm sure on Judgement Day lovers of wine-cup awake

from death's sleep… "Winebringer, more… to slake!"

O Zauq, if you have taste, from this world be

escaping...

this house of madness is not a fit place for the

uniting!

I will be staying in that shadow of Your

mansion…

what can a sinner like me do in paradise:

mention!

I looked for You far and wide, up and down in
vain…
when I finally found You I had vanished once
again!

By refusing to offer praise to Adam, Satan lost

all…

if he was to now bow a thousand times he'd still

fall!

Long before pigeon arrived my note reached

You

on the wings of my anxiety and my love for

You!